My dad is the owner of The Green Kettle. He's the chef there. A chef's job is cooking.

Today I'm going to work with Dad. We live only a few blocks from where Dad works, so I told him I wanted to walk.

It's very cold, so we are hurrying. I can't wait to get to The Green Kettle because I'm sure it'll be nice and warm there.

Dad talks about work a lot. He says being his own boss is fun and that he likes seeing all the people who come in. One of the things Dad's making today is soup. He says we'll make it together and that it'll be fun.

I don't know what's so much fun about making soup, but I suppose I'll find out.

"This is my workplace," Dad said cheerfully, stretching his arms out as if he was going to hug the whole room!

"So what kind of soup should we make today?" he asked. "You get to choose."

"You mean that I'm the boss today?" I asked.

Dad smiled and handed me a white chef's hat. "In a way," he said.

Dad found a cookbook and brought it over to a
long table in the middle of the room.

We opened the book to SOUPS and started looking
through it.

"Apple soup?" I said. "Yuck. Bean soup. Double yuck."

Then we came to the ones starting with the letter C and
I found chicken soup.

"Finally," I said, "something I like."

"Chicken soup it is," said Dad. "Now off we go to the
supermarket to get what we need to make it."

As Dad was picking out some of the veggies we needed, he said, "Choose some of those turnips."

When I took a turnip from the middle of the pile, many others starting falling all around me! A store clerk peered at me over her glasses as I picked them up.

Next we went to buy some fresh bread to serve with the soup. While Dad ordered, I drummed on the square tiles of the counter until Dad gave me a look.

After that we went to pick out a few chickens.

1.59

1.79

25¢

When we were ready to go, Dad reached for the two huge bags. I said I'd carry them, but no matter what I did, I couldn't get both arms all the way around the bags. Dad laughed and took one of the bags. I took the other one.

"We make a good team," I said.

The first thing we did when we got back to The Green Kettle was rinse the dirt from the veggies. We also rinsed the chickens. Dad said the cook always gets rinsed too, so he squirted me with water.

Next we filled a large pot with water. I've never seen a pot so big. I guess Dad thinks a lot of people are coming to The Green Kettle tonight.

Dad told me that cooking can have a lot of steps. "With our soup," he said, "the first step is to make the chicken stock."

Dad let me add the carrots. Plop, plop, plop, plop. After he added the chickens, he put the lid on the pot and said, "That's Step One. Now the stock needs to cook for two hours."

Then Dad said, "Now for Step Two." We chopped up some carrots, turnips, and shallots. Dad put them in a pan with butter. To stir them, he just tossed everything in the air and the veggies flipped by themselves. Dad let me try once.

Then Dad crumbled some parsley and sprinkled it in. I added salt and pepper. Once everything was cooked, it went into the soup.

For Step Three, we made the noodles. They boiled in a big pot.

"When they wiggle, they're cooked," said Dad.

"They're wiggling, Dad," I said.

"I've got the strainer," said Dad. Then he took the noodles out and dropped them into the soup pot.

"Step Four," Dad said. "A good cook always takes the first taste, but blow on it first. It's going to be very hot!"

"Perfect," I said, as I tried the soup.

Dad also took some and said, "The best."

Then at last it was time to serve the soup.

"The soup of the day is chicken soup, made by two great chefs!" the waiter said to some people who had come for dinner.

"Thank the chefs for us," said one of them.

"This is the best chicken soup I've ever had," said the other.